JESSE
OWENS

by
Wayne Coffey

BLACKBIRCH PRESS, INC.
Woodbridge, Connecticut

Published by Blackbirch Press, Inc.
One Bradley Road
Woodbridge, CT 06525

©1992 Blackbirch Press, Inc.
First Edition

Manufactured in the United States of America

Editor: Bruce Glassman
Photo Research: Grace How
Illustration: Mike Eagle

Library of Congress Cataloging-in-Publication Data

Coffey, Wayne R.
   Jesse Owens / Wayne Coffey. — 1st ed.
   (Olympic Gold)
   Includes bibliographical references and index.
   Summary: A biography of the track star who overcame childhood illness and racial prejudice to win four gold medals in the 1936 Olympics.
   ISBN 1-56711-000-2
   1. Owens, Jesse, 1913-   —Juvenile literature. 2. Track and field athletes—United States—Biography—Juvenile literature. [1. Owens, Jesse, 1913- . 2. Track and field athletes. 3. Afro-Americans—Biography.] I. Title. II. Series.
GV697.09C64 1992
796.42 ' 092—dc20
[B]
                             92-5206
                                CIP
                                AC

Contents

A Young Boy Struggles with Pain

"I want to be able to run like my father."

When Jesse Owens was a young boy, he loved to watch his father run. Jesse marveled at how his graceful strides seemed to gobble up the ground. Most folks agreed that Henry Owens, a lean, muscular man, was the fastest runner in the whole county.

Henry Owens usually ran on Sundays, when the men in town gathered after church. While other neighbors visited each other or sang gospel songs, the runners would race, pumping their arms and churning their legs, trying their hardest to finish first. But first place almost always belonged to Henry Owens.

Opposite:
As a young boy, Jesse was inspired by his father's natural grace and speed.

The races would make young Jesse very proud. There was something beautiful about running that fast. It seemed so natural, so free. It made Jesse dream about growing up to be strong and athletic, too.

Problems with Health

That dream seemed very far off for Jesse. He had many health problems as a child. He had constant bouts with pneumonia. He suffered high fevers and terrible coughing spells. There were many times when Henry and Emma Owens worried that their little boy would not survive.

Jesse fought back from his illnesses. He was determined to get better. "Someday, I want to be able to run like my father," he would say to himself.

The truth is that Jesse Owens didn't grow up to be just the fastest man in the county. He did his father one better. He grew up to be the fastest man in the world!

James Cleveland Owens was born on September 12, 1913, in the little town of Oakville, in northern Alabama. His parents and his six brothers and sisters called him by his initials, J.C. A few years later, on his first day in a new school after the family moved north, the teacher asked the new arrival his name.

"J.C., ma'am," the boy replied.

"Welcome to the class, Jesse," the teacher said warmly. J.C. was too shy to correct his teacher, especially on the first day. Besides, he kind of liked his new name. It was the name he would use for the rest of his life.

> *There was something beautiful about running that fast. It seemed so natural, so free. It made Jesse dream about growing up to be strong and athletic, too.*

The Owens family faced many hard times in Oakville. Jesse's parents were sharecroppers, picking cotton on a big farm owned by a wealthy white man named John Clannon. Henry and Emma Owens often worked from sunrise to sunset. So did their children. Jesse started working the cotton fields at age six. Such hard work was not the best thing for his fragile health. But the family didn't have much choice.

A Life of Poverty

Like many black families, the Owenses lived in constant poverty. As hard as they worked, it was almost impossible for them to get ahead. They earned only pennies each week for all their toil. But there were few jobs available to black people in the south at that time. And because there were no formal schools for black children, the families didn't have education as a way to improve their situation.

Often there wasn't enough food to go around. Meals would usually be made of

7

potatoes, beans, or corn. Mrs. Owens grew these things in a tiny vegetable patch behind their living quarters. Twice a year—at Easter and Christmas—the family would treat themselves to a ham.

The Owens home was more a hut than a house. It was made out of cardboard and a few planks. The roof leaked badly. There was no stove or bathroom—not even any running water. When winter came and the weather turned colder, the chill would blow right into the little shack. On the cold nights, Mrs. Owens made sure her ailing son, J.C., was wrapped in a blanket. She would lay her child closest to the fireplace to keep him warm.

The Owens home was more a hut than a house. It was made out of cardboard and a few planks. The roof leaked badly. There was no stove or bathroom—not even running water.

The conditions made it very difficult for Jesse to get well. Mrs. Owens cared for her son, giving him comfort and some homemade remedies. But the family couldn't afford to buy medicines from a store. And there weren't any doctors in Oakville.

A Turn for the Worse

The young boy's health worsened in the winter of 1919. The pneumonia made its annual attack, sapping Jesse of what little strength he had. As if that were not enough, he also developed a painful growth on his

left leg. Everyone hoped it would go away on its own, but it only grew larger and more painful. Jesse was afraid. Walking became more and more difficult. His mother gently rubbed the leg and applied hot washcloths. But none of the treatments seemed to help.

At the age of six, Jesse developed a painful growth on his leg. His mother finally had to remove it herself.

Mrs. Owens felt there was no choice but to try to remove the growth. She prepared young Jesse as best she could. "This is going to hurt, J.C.," she told him. "But your mama has got to do it for your own good." One of J.C.'s brothers held him as Emma Owens clutched a sharp knife and carefully

9

cut into the growth. Pain pulsed through the little boy's body. It seemed as if it would never end. He had never felt more pain in his whole life.

Jesse's leg healed quickly, but his health problems remained. He became so ill in the winter of 1921 that he was regularly coughing up blood.

Plans to Move

Deeply worried about their son, Henry and Emma Owens talked about leaving Oakville. They were convinced that unless they lived in a better place, with better medical care, J.C. might not survive. They had discussed moving north before, but never put a plan into action.

Life was very hard in Oakville; the Owenses didn't doubt that for a moment. But was it hard enough to take the risk of moving? What if things got worse up north?

Finally, they decided to take the chance. They sold their farm tools and their five mules, which earned them a small amount of money for the trip. They gathered their battered belongings and boarded a train.

The destination was Cleveland, Ohio, an industrial city near Lake Erie. Jesse was eight years old. He didn't know it then, but the move was going to be one of the best things that ever happened to him.

The Gift of Speed

"Who is that kid? And where did he learn to run like that?"

esse's new life in Cleveland was so different, it was almost as if he'd stumbled onto a new planet. Clanging trolley cars motored up and down big, noisy streets. There were tall buildings and big factories. Huge freighters steamed across the Great Lakes, carrying goods to distant places. At night, neon signs flashed and lighted up the dark sky. The Owens family settled on the city's east side, where there were many stores—and more people—than Jesse had ever seen before.

The biggest difference for Jesse was that, for the first time, he was a full-time student. Instead of picking cotton, he was opening books. He attended St. Clair's Grammar School on St. Clair Avenue. He worked at reading and writing. He learned about arithmetic and science. Because he had no formal schooling, Jesse had to work hard to catch up to the other students. Sometimes he got frustrated. But his parents stressed the importance of good education, and he was eager to learn as much as he could. Without schooling, it would be hard to get a good job when he grew up. Henry Owens, who hadn't had a chance to go to school, was a perfect example of someone who suffered from little education.

A New Life in Cleveland

The move to Cleveland did little to ease the family's money problems. It was hard for Henry Owens to find steady work. He swept floors and washed windows. Other times, he took on factory work. Mrs. Owens worked as a cleaning woman. Along with his brothers and sisters, Jesse helped in any way he could. He would rush home from school, then go off to work at a gas station or as a delivery boy. Some days, he would carry groceries for people. Or he would deliver flowers or shine shoes. If anybody in the neighborhood needed to have an errand done, Jesse was ready to do it.

For the first time [Jesse] was a full-time student. Instead of picking cotton he was opening books.

Though he remained as thin as a post, young Jesse's health improved steadily. He loved to run and play with his friends during recess at school. And the more he ran, the more he discovered that, like his dad, he was blessed with the gift of speed.

A Coach Takes Notice

One day at recess, a group of youngsters were dashing across the schoolyard. They caught the eye of a man named Charles Riley, a gym teacher at the school. Mr. Riley also served as the track coach at nearby Fairmont Junior High School and East Technical High School. Mr. Riley was a seasoned track-and-field observer. He was startled by the skinny kid at the head of the pack, moving like a puma. The track coach had seen many speedy runners in his time. But there was something special about the way this youngster was racing.

"Who is that kid?" Mr. Riley wondered. "And where did he learn to run like that?"

Mr. Riley approached Jesse and introduced himself. "Would you be interested in joining our school track team?" he asked.

Jesse's eyes widened. He had never been on a track team before. He nodded with excitement.

"Great," Mr. Riley said. "We have practices after school."

Suddenly, Jesse's enthusiasm vanished. There was no way he could attend practices after school. That was when he worked to help earn money for the family. It looked as if his track career might be over before it began.

Mr. Riley taught [Jesse] to run lightly, almost as if he were floating over the ground.

But Mr. Riley had an idea. He asked Jesse if he would be willing to get to school early for a 45-minute workout every morning. That wouldn't interfere with anything, except a little sleep. Jesse would just go to bed a little earlier. Jesse loved the idea.

Progress was slow at first. As much natural talent as he had, Jesse had to learn the finer points of running. He had to learn about using his arms to increase his speed, and starting as fast as possible. Mr. Riley taught him to run lightly, almost as if he were floating over the ground. Jesse also had to get into top physical condition to endure his demanding workouts.

The coach and the young runner formed a close bond. Mr. Riley became like a second father to Jesse. But even so, it was hard for Jesse to constantly train alone. Often Jesse became discouraged, because he didn't feel his running was improving very much. When he told Mr. Riley about his feelings, the coach urged him to be patient. The best things in life take time, Mr.

Riley explained. The challenge is to stick with it, not to give up. When you do that, in the end, you will have an accomplishment that will make you proud.

Whenever Mr. Riley sensed Jesse getting impatient, the coach would smile and say, "You're training for four years from next Friday." It was the coach's amusing way of keeping Jesse focused on his long-term goals. And it worked. Jesse couldn't help but smile when Mr. Riley said it.

Jesse's First Track Meet

Even if Jesse wasn't always satisfied with his progress, Mr. Riley certainly was. He saw a prize-winning pupil getting better and better. By the time young Jesse enrolled at Fairmont Junior High, he was ready to compete in an organized school track meet.

Jesse competed in his first track meet when he was in his first year at Fairmont Junior High School.

There were rivals from numerous other schools in the area. Jesse had never seen most of them before. He wondered how fast they were and how he would measure up against them. When he thought about it, his heart raced in anticipation. He felt his hands go cold and clammy. From head to track shoe, Jesse felt nervous—a feeling he would have before almost every competition, for as long as he ran.

Finally, it was time for the 100-yard dash to begin. Jesse and the other runners took their places at the starting line, ready to explode into a sprint when the gun sounded.

Bang! Off went the gun and the pack of runners. One hundred yards later, the first to cross the finish line, by a wide margin, was the skinny kid from Fairmont Junior High. Jesse beamed and raced over to Mr. Riley, who was as proud as a new father.

Mr. Riley told Emma Owens, "Your son has the most unusual pair of legs on this earth. I know this will shock you, but Jesse could become an Olympic champion."

There would be hundreds more victories in Jesse Owens' career. But there would never be another first victory.

Afterward, Mr. Riley told a proud Emma Owens, "Your son has the most unusual pair of legs on this earth. I know this will shock you, but Jesse could become an Olympic champion."

Jesse couldn't get enough of track and field. He started running on the relay team.

He trained to run the 220-yard dash. He also tried the hurdles, which require not only speed, but exact timing. In the hurdles, runners must jump over a series of gates that can be more than three feet high. Every event Jesse tried, he dominated.

Jesse's First American Track Record

There seemed to be no stopping him. One meet, while Jesse was at Fairmont, was truly unforgettable. He won the 100-yard dash in 10 seconds flat. No junior high school athlete in history had ever run so fast. Jesse Owens had earned his first American record.

The following day, the Cleveland newspapers reported the feat. People began to talk about the awesome young talent from the city's east side. They wondered how much faster he might become, as he grew and added more muscle and learned more about the strategies of running.

Jesse and Mr. Riley wondered the same thing. But they didn't want to get ahead of themselves. The most important thing was just to keep working at it, every day. Do your best for today, and think about tomorrow when tomorrow comes. The big race, Jesse always reminded himself, is four years from next Friday.

3

A Chance for
a Better Life

*"He doesn't want money.
He wants to work."*

As he moved on to East Technical High School, Jesse began competing against the best high school runners and jumpers in Cleveland. Some young athletes have difficulty when they move up to tougher competition. They find that they don't perform as well as they used to. Or they discover that their rate of improvement slows down while their rivals continue to get better.

Jesse had no problems with the adjustment. He aced the sprints and hurdles, and before long, he was a star in the broad jump, too. In the broad jump, athletes sprint down a 140-foot runway. Then, when they get to a takeoff board, they jump forward as far as they can into a pit. The pit is full of sand to cushion their fall.

All through high school, Jesse followed a busy schedule. He kept up with his schoolwork. He took on any job he could find to help the family. And he trained hard with Mr. Riley.

Word of Jesse Owens Spreads

With Mr. Riley's constant support and guidance, Jesse's track exploits drew more and more attention. The first-place finishes were becoming almost routine. Just as his father had done years before in Alabama, young Jesse was becoming known for having the fastest legs in Cleveland.

One day in 1933, Jesse's reputation really took off. The East Technical High team was invited to the National Interscholastic Championships. The big meet was hosted by the University of Chicago. Top teams and top athletes from around the country were invited to attend. College coaches rushed to the event, hoping to recruit the best young talents for their schools. The stands were packed with spectators and the press. It was the biggest, toughest competition Jesse Owens had ever entered.

All through high school, Jesse followed a busy schedule. He kept up with his schoolwork. He took on any job he could find to help the family.

19

In 1933, Jesse set a new high-school record for the 100-yard dash. He also won the 220-yard dash and the broad jump in the same competition in Chicago.

A One-Man Show

When it was over, one name stood out above all the others. Jesse Owens had won the 100-yard dash in 9.4 seconds, setting a new world high-school record. He won the 220-yard dash in 20.7 seconds. He won the broad jump with a leap of 24 feet, 9⅝ inches. A group of Jesse's East Technical teammates had also competed at the meet. But if ever there was a one-man show, this was it.

People couldn't stop talking about Jesse Owens. In praising his feats in *The New York Times,* sportswriter Joseph Sheehan

called the effort "an unprecedented triple."
About the only thing Jesse Owens didn't do
in Chicago was swim across Lake Michigan!

Another Love

Nobody was more taken with Jesse than a
young woman named Ruth Solomon. She
met Jesse shortly after he moved from
Oakville, and they began dating in junior
high school. Ruth was a kind, sensitive
person. The more Jesse spent time with her,
the more interested he became. He always
felt very special when he was around Ruth.
Before the young couple left high school,
they decided to be married.

It didn't take long for scholarship offers
to start pouring in. Schools with the most
elite track-and-field teams in the country
sought out Jesse. The offers were worth
thousands of dollars apiece. Jesse was
assured of living like a king, compared with
what he was used to. His home would be
on a campus with big, impressive buildings. All his meals would be paid for. His
books, his tuition, his living expenses—
they too would all be covered!

The attention was flattering, but Jesse
became overwhelmed. Nobody in the
Owens family had ever even attended
college, never mind being awarded a scholarship. Throughout his life, Jesse had only

known poverty. The whole family worked, and even then, the Owenses just barely scraped by. What's more, Henry Owens had just lost his job working in a factory. It only paid $12 a week, but it was a major blow to the family.

Too Many Choices

The more Jesse thought about college, the more troubled he became. "How can I go off to some expensive college when my own family doesn't even have enough to eat?" Jesse worried.

Finally, Jesse made up his mind. He told Mr. Riley that he couldn't accept any of the offers. In fact, with his dad out of work, Jesse decided he had to quit the East Technical track team, too. He felt very confused, but his decision was firm. The family had to come first.

Mr. Riley was stunned. He understood the difficult problem Jesse had. And he knew what a responsible young man Jesse was. But the decision still saddened Mr. Riley. Not only would it mean the end of Jesse's track career, it would mean missing a chance to get a college education. And a good education, Mr. Riley knew, would be the best way for Jesse to insure a better life for himself.

No one in the Owens family had ever even attended college, never mind being awarded a scholarship.

There was just one hope. Mr. Riley asked Jesse, "If I could get your father a steady job, would you go to college?"

Henry Owens had never held a steady job. Jesse thought such a thing didn't exist for a black man with no education. Besides, with the country slipping into the Great Depression, the odds for work got worse. The Depression was a terrible economic slump in the 1930s. It caused thousands of people to lose their jobs and homes.

Mr. Riley pressed his point. "If there were a job for your father, would you reconsider your decision?" the coach asked.

Jesse paused for several moments. "Yes, I guess I would," he said.

A Special Coach in Columbus

It was just the answer Mr. Riley was hoping to hear. With that, he was off on a 150-mile trip to Columbus, the home of Ohio State University. Mr. Riley went to talk with Larry Snyder, the coach of the Ohio State track team. Larry Snyder was regarded as one of the best track-and-field coaches in the United States.

Mr. Snyder listened keenly to his visitor. He explained to Mr. Riley that Ohio State did not offer athletic scholarships. Jesse Owens would have to pay his own expenses, just as the other students did.

"He doesn't want money," Mr. Riley said. "He wants to work. And he wants to find work for his father, too."

Mr. Snyder smiled. He thought something could possibly be done. He talked to top school officials about the matter.

By the time Mr. Riley left Columbus a couple of days later, he was carrying two letters. Both were addressed to Jesse Owens. One letter was an official welcome, for he had been admitted to the university. It explained that he would be able to meet his schooling expenses by working various jobs on campus.

The second letter revealed that Henry Owens was wanted for a job with the state of Ohio. It was a guaranteed job, no matter what happened to his son's track career.

It was one of the best days of Jesse's life. He would be going to college after all! After he finished reading the letters, Jesse just held them in his fist as he stood in front of Mr. Riley. It's hard to say who was happier. Jesse was quiet for a few moments, as he struggled to find the rights words to say.

A feeling of warmth and gratitude swept over Jesse. He still wasn't sure what he wanted to say. Then, without really thinking about it, he took a step forward. Jesse Owens wrapped his arms around Charles Riley and gave him a big kiss.

4

The Shadow of Prejudice

"You're not really running against other people . . . you're running against yourself."

One of the smartest moves Larry Snyder ever made was helping Jesse Owens get admitted to Ohio State. Jesse lived up to every expectation, and more. Before long, people around Columbus were calling him "The Brown Bombshell." Others called him "The Buckeye Bullet." The Ohio State sports teams were nicknamed the Buckeyes. And Jesse was fast and explosive, like a human bullet.

Being a student at a university was challenging and eye-opening. The schoolwork was more demanding than any he had done before. Jesse worked three jobs to pay his way through school. He had a job in the library. He waited on tables in a cafeteria. And at night he operated a freight elevator. When there wasn't much freight, Jesse would crack open one of his schoolbooks and catch up on his reading.

The Cruelty of Prejudice

College was a great time for Jesse in many ways. He was getting an education. He was traveling to new places. Under the expert eye of Larry Snyder, his running progressed steadily. But Jesse experienced one very troubling thing too: racial prejudice. Whites simply did not give blacks equal rights in the world. And many whites were often cruel to blacks.

Jesse knew such injustices existed, of course. He had grandparents who were slaves. He also had vivid memories of the sharecropping life in Oakville. The family worked long and hard to squeeze out a living only to give half their earnings to the wealthy white man who owned the land.

An Incident in Indiana

The sting of prejudice was painful. It hurt Jesse to feel prejudice at the same time he was being hailed as the "Buckeye Bullet." The worst episode came on a February morning in Indiana. The Ohio State team was traveling through southern Indiana, heading for a track meet in Indianapolis. The sun was just coming up over the lush farmland, as one little town after another began to stir.

The sting of prejudice was painful. It hurt Jesse to feel prejudice at the same time he was being hailed as the "Buckeye Bullet."

The team had been driving for several hours. The athletes were getting hungry. Mr. Snyder, riding in the lead car, pulled over by a small roadside diner. The other cars pulled over, too. Coach Snyder and the white team members piled out of their cars and went inside. Jesse and his three black teammates stayed in Jesse's old Ford. Jesse was very familiar with this routine.

Mr. Snyder was talking to a woman behind the counter. The conversation became heated. Then Mr. Snyder stomped out of the diner toward the Ford. He had tried to convince the woman to let the blacks eat breakfast with their white teammates.

The counterwoman said no. "The owner isn't around right now," she said. "I can't take that responsibility."

A few minutes later, after downing a quick breakfast, Mr. Snyder and the whites came out of the diner. They were carrying plates of food. There were fried eggs and a thick stack of fresh toast. By now Jesse and his friends were starving. They had just started eating when a big man with a fat gut and a scowl appeared outside the car window. He was the owner of the diner.

"So this is why you wanted the extra food," the man shouted. "They told me it was for the white boys to eat on the road."

"You were paid, weren't you, mister?" said Ralph Metcalfe, one of Jesse's black teammates. (He was a track star in his own right, winning two medals in the 1932 Olympics.)

The owner's face reddened. His voice was even angrier now. "I don't want money to feed any niggers!" he said. Then, in an instant, the man's big, beefy hand reached through the window and grabbed for the food. He slammed his fist down on the

While traveling through southern Indiana one February, Jesse and his black Ohio State teammates experienced the cruelty of prejudice. When they stopped to eat at a diner, they were denied food because they were black.

plates. Eggs and toast flew all over the car. So did silverware. The man carried the plates back inside. The only food that was left was on the floor.

Jesse and his friends burned with rage. One of the young blacks jumped out of the car and was ready to fight the owner, but Jesse held him back. If a black man took a swing at a white man, there was no telling how much trouble he might find. Jesse saw tears in his friend's eyes. Jesse felt like crying himself.

At the track meet later that day, Jesse ran with a passion and fury he had never known before. He felt an extra surge of energy flowing through him. From beginning to end, he was the star of the competition. Fans streamed out of the stands to meet him and get his autograph. One man even asked Jesse to sign his Bible. Almost all of these fans were white. Jesse didn't hold this against them, just because it had been a white man who had treated him so horribly at the diner. He signed all the autographs. Jesse felt it was very important not to judge people merely by the color of their skin. He knew nice people come in all shapes, sizes, and races.

"If I punish these people just because they are white, I'm no better than the fat guy at the diner," Jesse told himself.

A Career Highlight

The highlight of Jesse's career at Ohio State came in May of 1935, at the University of Michigan. The meet was the National Collegiate Athletic Association Championships. Top track-and-field athletes from colleges around the country were all on hand.

Jesse almost had to miss the competition. Several days before, he had hurt his back while playing around with friends. His whole upper body was stiff. He felt a constant, jabbing pain. He applied heating pads and ointments. He soaked in a hot tub. He took off from practice, hoping rest would help. Even on the day of the meet, Jesse wasn't sure if he would be able to get into a crouch position for the start of a race.

In his pain, Jesse remembered something Mr. Riley used to tell him. "You're not really running against other people," Mr. Riley believed. "You're running against yourself. Your goal is to do your very best, every time out. It's to push yourself to your limit. The great athlete is the one who doesn't stop when his legs start to hurt or he's out of breath," Mr. Riley said. "The great athlete has the discipline and inner strength to keep going. He or she doesn't give up."

Even with an aching back, Jesse did not give up. He was determined not to let his injury get in his way. And his reward was what one sportswriter called "the greatest day in track history." Jesse matched his own world record of 9.4 seconds in the 100-yard dash. He set a world record in the 220-yard dash, running it in 20.3 seconds. He set another world mark in the 220-yard low hurdles, with a clocking of 22.6 seconds.

And the broad jump? Jesse didn't just break a world record. He smashed it. His jump was measured at 26 feet, 8¼ inches— a feat so amazing that the record stood for 25 years! The huge crowd at the University of Michigan was in awe. The fans cheered wildly. They knew they had witnessed a historic performance.

Jesse felt it was very important not to judge people merely by the color of their skin. He knew nice people come in all shapes, sizes, and races.

As thrilled as he was with his results, Jesse did not let up with his training. In fact, he practiced harder than ever. He knew the biggest challenge of his athletic career— the Olympic Games—was still ahead of him.

5

The Dream Comes True

"I've had people cheer for me, but never like that."

By 1936, Jesse was the most famous amateur athlete in the United States. The whole country was counting on him to run and jump his best in the upcoming Olympics. He would be going up against the greatest athletes from all over the world. That was a scary thought, but not nearly as scary as the thought those other athletes had. They were going up against Jesse Owens.

Jesse was stunned by what he saw when he arrived in Berlin, Germany, for the 1936 Olympic Games. There were impressive new buildings throughout the capital city.

32

(Continued on page 49)

1936

BERLIN, GERMANY

COLLEGE TRACK STAR

While at Ohio State University, Jesse became a track-and-field superstar. At this meet in Ann Arbor, Michigan, in 1935, he broke a record for the 220-yard dash that had stood for nine years. *Opposite top:* At Ohio State, Jesse perfected a new style for starting a race. On the left, he shows the traditional start position. On the right, he shows his standing start, which was first suggested to him by his high school coach, Charles Riley. *Opposite bottom:* Jesse stands with his Ohio State coach, Larry Snyder.

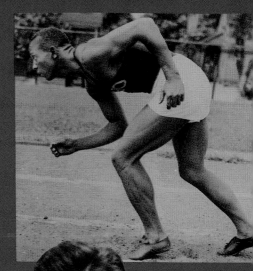

COMPETITION IN GERMANY

Olympic Stadium in Berlin, 1936, on the first day of the Games. *Inset:* A poster printed by the German government to promote the Olympics.

DEUTSCHLAND

XI. OLYMPIADE
BERLIN
1936

HITLER'S OLYMPICS

Above: Adolph Hitler leads Olympic officials at the Berlin stadium. *Left:* The Olympic flag flies alongside the Nazi flag in Germany, 1936. *Opposite:* Hitler greets German citizens during the Olympic Games. Hitler hoped that the 1936 Olympics would show the world that the Aryan (Nordic) race was superior to all others.

JUMPING RECORD

Jesse, as he set an Olympic broad jump record of 26 feet, 5½ inches. His gold medal effort remained unequalled for 24 years.

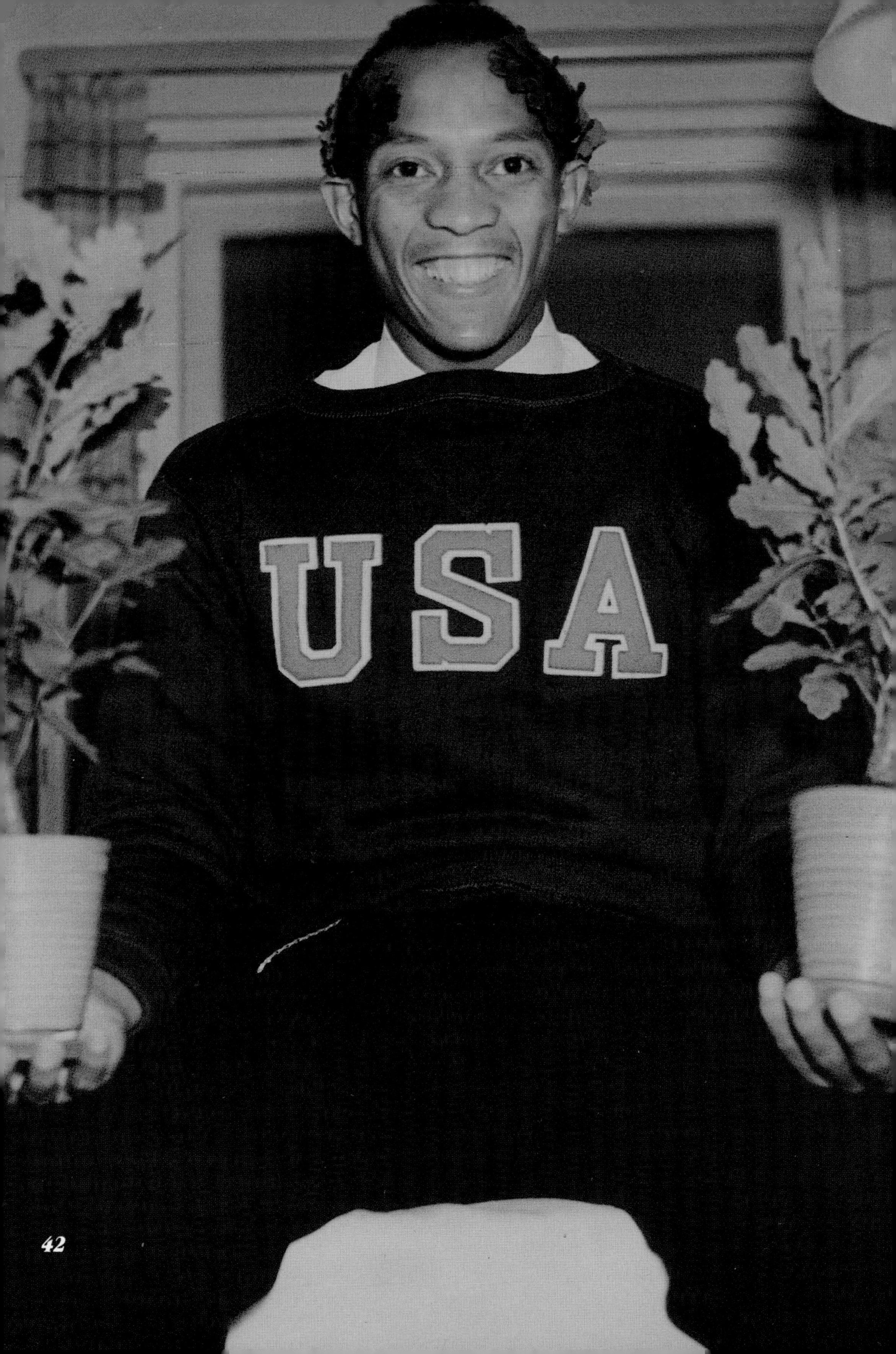
USA

FRUITS OF VICTORY

Opposite: Jesse smiles with his first two Olympic oaks, given to
winners of medals. These oaks were given to him after his gold medal
wins in the 100-meter dash and the broad jump. He went on to win
the gold for the 200-meter dash and as a member of the victorious
4 x 100-meter relay team. *Below:* Jesse stands with his gold medal
relay teammates in Berlin's Olympic Stadium. Together, the four men
established a new Olympic record with a race of 39.8 seconds. From
left are Jesse, Ralph Metcalfe, Foy Draper, and Frank Wykoff.

HONOR AND GLORY

At the awards ceremony for the broad jump, Jesse stands on the platform behind bronze medal winner, Tajima of Japan. Behind Jesse is silver medal winner, Luz Long of Germany. Luz Long and Jesse met at the Berlin Olympics and became good friends.

A Hero's Welcome

Above: A massive parade in New York honors Jesse upon his return from Berlin in September of 1936.
Right: Jesse and his wife Ruth enjoy the adoration of the crowd as they return to their hometown of Cleveland, Ohio. There, Jesse was given a giant parade that covered more than 12 miles.

SPORTS AMBASSADOR

Later in his life, Jesse remained active in helping and promoting the Olympic Games. He served as director of the U.S. Olympic committee and organized a Canadian coin program that raised thousands of dollars for the 1976 Games in Montreal.

(Continued from page 32)

The facilities were all first-rate. The shining Olympic stadium, where Jesse would be competing, was the biggest place he had ever seen. It held more than 100,000 people.

It seemed that the entire country was assembled for the celebration. Orchestras played the music of German composers. Tens of thousands of young soldiers marched all lined up in perfect rows.

Hitler's Olympics

Adolf Hitler, Germany's leader, was eager to use the Games to show off his country. Hitler was a powerful leader who used an army to rule by force and fear. As soon as he took power, he began arresting Jewish people and sending them to camps to be killed. He blamed Jews for almost every problem Germany had. Before he was finished, Adolf Hitler was responsible for killing more than 6 million Jews.

"The Führer" (leader), as Hitler was called, believed the Germans were a perfect race, superior to all other peoples. Germany was supposed to rule the world, Hitler said. Only three years after the Olympics, Hitler's invasion of Poland plunged the world into World War II, causing hundreds of thousands more deaths.

It was very important to Hitler that his German athletes dominate the Olympics.

Their victories would be the ultimate proof of German superiority. And he thought German athletes would prove how inferior blacks were. Hitler hated blacks the way he hated Jews. He went out of his way to snub the black Americans during the Games. In fact, as Jesse was about to begin competing in the broad jump, Hitler got up and left his seat. It was his way of telling Jesse, "You're not even worth watching."

Jesse was furious at the insult. "He'll hear about this jump, even if he doesn't see it!" Jesse told himself. But Jesse was too fired up for his own good and he had trouble focusing on his jumps. On his first attempt, he ran beyond the takeoff board, resulting in a foul. On his second attempt, he was so careful not to foul that he didn't go very far.

This was a competition to determine who would qualify for the broad jump finals.

Hitler hated blacks the way he hated Jews . . . As Jesse was about to begin competing in the broad jump, Hitler got up and left his seat.

Each jumper had three chances to qualify. Jesse had only one chance left. And the broad jump was really his best event. He had the world record by a huge margin. And now he was one jump away from not making it out of the qualifying round!

Jesse was getting more anxious by the second. He felt even more pressure after watching the jump of Luz Long. A tall, muscular, blond-haired German, Long was the second best long jumper in the world, behind Jesse Owens. He was also Hitler's shining example of the "master race theory." On his first jump, Luz Long soared to an Olympic record. The fans in the massive stadium roared with approval. Jesse had always tried to get off to a great start in competitions so that other athletes would get discouraged. Now Luz Long had discouraged Jesse.

Jesse prepared to take his third and final qualifying jump. His entire Olympic career was riding on this. If he failed in his best event, what could he expect to do in the others? Jesse began feeling panicky. He thought about his 10 years of training in the sport. He looked over at Hitler's empty box, and he gazed into the stands, where 100,000 people, almost all of them German, were hoping he would fail.

Jesse paced nervously. He felt his legs trembling in fear. He had never felt so afraid. In a moment, it would be his turn to jump again. Jesse Owens felt lost.

Kindness from a German Rival

Suddenly, there was a strong grip on Jesse's arm. He wheeled around. Standing before him was his German rival, Luz Long. Long looked at Jesse with his blazing blue eyes.

In the qualifying round
for the Olympic broad
jump, German athlete
Luz Long calmed
Jesse and offered him
kind advice.

"Hello, Jesse Owens," Long said. "I know
what a fine jumper you are. I want to see
you make the finals. It's important to relax
and remember you are only trying to qualify.
You don't need to be the best on this jump."

Luz Long then made a suggestion. He
told Jesse he should measure his steps on
the runway so he would take off six inches
behind the board. That way he would be in
no danger of fouling, and he would still
jump plenty far enough to qualify.

Jesse was speechless. He could hardly
believe a German was offering guidance
and kindness to a black American. But Luz
Long was right.

Jesse was very grateful for Long's help.
He could feel his panic ease and his muscles

relax. He measured his steps again. He placed a towel beside the runway, next to where he wanted to take off. Then Jesse sped down the approach and took off exactly where the towel was. Jesse qualified easily.

Battle for the Gold

The next day, in the finals, the battle for the gold medal came down to Jesse Owens and Luz Long. Jesse later called it "the most intense competition" of his life. Jesse set an Olympic record with his first jump. Long matched it. Back and forth they went, drama building each time one of them flew through the air into the sand.

On the fifth of his six jumps, Long leaped 25 feet, 10 inches—farther than he'd ever jumped in his life. Jesse responded by jumping just over 26 feet. Then he followed that with a jump of 26 feet, 5½ inches. It was short of Jesse's own world record, but it set an Olympic record.

The crowd was cheering in appreciation of the two greatest athletes. On his final jump, Luz Long gave it everything he had, but came up well short. Jesse Owens had won the gold medal. The first one to congratulate him was his new German friend, who grabbed Jesse's hand and walked him toward the stands.

Looking up into the vast sea of faces, Long held Jesse's hand over his head, and started chanting, "Jesse Owens, Jesse Owens." Soon the whole stadium was chanting the name Jesse Owens. One hundred thousand people were paying tribute to a black American. Wherever Adolf Hitler was, you can be sure he wasn't happy. "I've had people cheer for me, but never like that," Jesse said later.

Jesse's Olympic triumphs were just beginning. He went on to win the 100-meter dash in 10.3 seconds. He won the 200 meters, in 20.7 seconds, then won another first as the anchor man on a four-man relay team. By the time the Games closed, the champion among champions was Jesse Owens, who had won four gold medals. He had arrived in Berlin with $7.40 in his pocket. The money was gone now, but he was rich beyond measure. He had secured a place in Olympic history. He had put forth an unforgettable performance.

Soon the whole stadium was chanting the name Jesse Owens. One hundred thousand people were paying tribute to a black American.

As he thought about it, Jesse could not forget the debt he owed Luz Long. Without Luz, it was possible that Jesse's victories might never have happened. The two spent hours and hours together during the Olympics, away from the arena. Both men were married and had a young child at home. They talked about their families. They talked about the race problems in America, and about Adolf Hitler.

Jesse Owens grew to love Luz Long. Saying goodbye to him was the hardest part of the Olympics for Jesse. How could Jesse ever forget the day that Luz reached out and gripped his arm, and helped him when he needed it most?

After three years of writing to each other, Jesse received a sad letter from his friend. Luz had joined the German army. "I am afraid, Jesse," Luz wrote. "I'm not afraid of dying, as much as dying for the wrong thing." Luz asked Jesse if he would visit his wife and son, in the event that Luz did not make it back home.

Jesse Loses a Friend

Jesse never received another letter from Luz. Jesse wrote back, but the letters kept being returned. He made calls and wrote more letters. He tried everything he could think of to find out if Luz was all right. There was no news. It was only years later that Jesse found out what happened. Luz Long had died in battle. He was buried in the African desert. It was some of the saddest news Jesse would ever hear. It was news Jesse would never forget.

6

Life After the Gold

*"There's too much hatred in the world.
We should treat each other as equals."*

Jesse's Olympic feats made him an American hero. In New York City, tens of thousands of people turned out to honor him in a ticker-tape parade. Millions of tiny bits of paper swirled in the air. People peered out of skyscraper windows to get a look at the man who proved Hitler wrong. The cheering was non-stop. Riding in a shiny new convertible, Jesse waved to his admirers until his arms hurt.

His picture was on the front page of every newspaper. People he didn't even know invited him to fancy parties. Wealthy businessmen insisted on taking him to dinner.

Jesse returned as a hero to America in 1936, after winning four gold medals in the Olympic Games.

Suddenly, Jesse was the toast of the yacht-and-limousine crowd!

Once the celebrations settled down, Jesse had more practical concerns. Ruth was pregnant with a second child. A few years later, they had a third child. Jesse needed to provide for his family. He couldn't help noticing that, while everybody was eager to shake his hand, nobody he met had offered him a job.

Jesse took a position with the recreation department in Cleveland. It didn't pay much, but it helped the family get by. Before long, he chose to pursue other opportunities. Jesse wanted to return to Ohio State to get his degree. With all the preparation he had done for the Olympics, he hadn't been able to keep up with his studies quite the way he wanted. Getting a college degree was important to Jesse.

New Business Efforts

Just as he competed in several different events in track, Jesse tried his hand at a variety of businesses. He went into the dry-cleaning business, with a successful chain of stores in Cleveland and other cities. The stores had a sign that said, "Speedy service from the world's fastest human." Jesse made a good deal of money over several years. Soon he had enough to buy new houses for his family, as well as for his parents. But his business was not without problems. Jesse found out he had a few dishonest partners. When the stores eventually went out of business, Jesse had to take care of the debts himself.

Jesse then worked as a salesman for several different companies. In Detroit, he was hired by Ford Motor Company to help recruit workers to make goods for the United States' war effort. Eventually, Jesse and his family settled in Chicago. He discovered that what he liked best, and did best, was working with kids and talking to people of all ages about his many experiences. He was a natural public-relations man. He had an easy smile and a friendly manner, and he had many fascinating stories to tell.

The "Ambassador of Sports"

In the early 1950s, Jesse was the head of a sports commission that helped troubled boys. He helped design programs to keep the boys busy with athletics and away from mischief. Later, the United States government asked if he would go overseas on a "goodwill trip." He was given the title "Ambassador of Sports." Jesse visited India and was a big hit. He told stories about his childhood, the Olympics, and, of course, about his friend, Luz Long. "He coached Indian athletes, spoke at schools and generally charmed everybody in sight," *Life* magazine wrote in an article.

> *He spoke not only about athletics, but about ideals: about the importance of honesty and fairness, and being open minded.*

Jesse kept a busy schedule. He loved going around the country, meeting people and giving talks. He spoke not only about athletics, but about ideals: about the importance of honesty and fairness, and being open-minded. Jesse suffered great hardships growing up as a poor black child in the south. He talked about not giving up when things were tough. He talked about racial injustice. He told people about that winter morning in Indiana, when the diner owner slammed his fist down and said he didn't want to feed any "niggers." One of Jesse's firm beliefs was that people shouldn't be judged by their religion or race. "There's too much hatred in the world," Jesse would say. "We should treat each other with kindness. We should treat each other as equals." Jesse believed when you have this attitude, you'll always have friends. And he believed that you'll never know when you'll make new ones.

Even as the decades passed, nobody could forget the achievements of Jesse Owens in Berlin in 1936. He was voted the greatest track athlete in the first 50 years of the twentieth century. When Gloria Owens, the oldest daughter of Jesse and Ruth Owens, was named Homecoming Queen of Ohio State University, Jesse returned to the stadium that was the site of so many of his triumphs. He received a tremendous ovation from the 82,000 fans. Later, when the university built a new track-and-field facility, it was named in his honor.

Jesse was named to the Track-and-Field Hall of Fame. He was awarded an honorary doctorate degree from Ohio State. He also earned a presidential medal of freedom for his contributions to America.

On March 30, 1980, James Cleveland Owens, whom everyone knew as Jesse, died of cancer at the age of 66. His death sparked many more tributes. There were monuments built in his hometown of Oakville, Alabama, and also in Cleveland. There was an outpouring of love for Jesse around the country. In Berlin, outside Olympic Stadium, a new street sign was erected. It said, "Jesse Owens Strasse." *Strasse* is the German word for street.

Jesse's Spirit Lives On

In 1984, as the Olympic Games were beginning in Los Angeles, a young woman named Gina Hemphill carried the Olympic torch into the jam-packed stadium. Gina Hemphill is Jesse Owen's granddaughter. Around the track she ran with the torch, then climbed the stadium steps to light the flame.

The flame represents the spirit of the Olympic Games—the ideals of sportsmanship and competition. At the Games, the greatest athletes in the world gather to compete for honor and glory. Most people that year agreed that the Olympics could not have picked a better torch-carrier than the granddaughter of Jesse Owens.

Glossary

amateur   An athlete who does not compete for money.

ambassador   An authorized representative.

Aryan race   A term used by Hitler to mean Caucasian people of non-Jewish descent.

depression   A period of time when business, employment, and stock market values decline or maintain a low level of activity.

economy   The earnings, debts, and production of a nation.

feat   A noteworthy achievement usually requiring skill or boldness.

Führer   German word for leader.

hurdle   A gate or barrier runners must jump over in certain races.

Nazi party   Political party that came under Hitler's control in Germany in 1933.

pneumonia   Inflammation of the lungs caused by bacteria or viruses.

poverty   The condition or quality of being poor.

racial prejudice   Intolerance or hatred of people of other races.

rival   One who competes against another.

scholarship   Money or aid granted to a student to pursue his or her studies.

Strasse   German word for street.

Further Reading

Arnold, Caroline. *The Olympic Summer Games.* New York: Franklin Watts, 1991.

Arnold, Caroline. *The Olympic Winter Games.* New York: Franklin Watts, 1991.

Bailey, Donna. *Track and Field.* Austin: Raintree Steck-Vaughn, 1991.

Huggins, Nathan Irvin. *Jesse Owens: Champion Athlete.* Broomall: Chelsea House, 1988.

Tatlow, Peter. *The Olympics.* New York: Franklin Watts, 1988.

Index

Photo Credits
Cover: Wide World Photos
Pages 33–37: Wide World Photos; page 38 (top): UPI/
Bettman; page 38 (bottom): Wide World Photos; page 39:
UPI/Bettman; pages 40–48: Wide World Photos.